The Adventures of Artie The Alphabet Cone

Book written by
Evan J. Schmidt

Editor: Daniella Schmidt

Illustrated by: Shafiakanwal93

First Edition 2022
ISBN: 9798357201003
www.artiethealphabetcone.com
Eeveeocean@gmail.com

Disclaimer: This is a work of creative nonfiction.
Some parts have been fictionalized in
varying degrees, for various purposes.

The characters in this book are entirely fictional.
This book's purpose is to educate, inform,
instruct and entertain. While the characters
are fictional it should be helpful.

No book can tell you everything that you want to know
or need to know about the topics it tries to cover.

The Adventures of Artie The Alphabet Cone

Collecting Seashells and Ocean Treasures A to Z

This book is dedicated to my family for helping me pursue my love for seashells.

Book written by
Evan J. Schmidt

Editor: Daniella Schmidt
Illustrated by: Shafiakanwal93

Hi there!

My name is Artie the Alphabet Cone. I am so excited you are here to explore the beach with me. I can't wait for you to learn about some of my favorite seashells and start your own seashell collection!

I am going to take you on an adventure to show you some of the seashells and other treasures you can find at the beach as well as learn about some of the animals that live inside them.

There are so many interesting things that wash up on beaches all over the world. So no matter what beach you visit, you will always find something special!

The ocean is made up of many sea creatures, animals, plants and shells. It's fun to collect these items to add to your seashell collection but some you may want to observe and enjoy in their natural habitat.

What we find today can be found in many oceans around the world. What is amazing is that every seashell and ocean creature is one of a kind just like you.

I love adventures! I have been on my own since the hurricane Rose swept me out to sea away from my home in Cone City. I have met so many new ocean friends on my journey home. I am having fun meeting and helping new friends along the way. There are so many new things to learn about our oceans and the animals that live in it.

Let's get started on our beach shelling adventure together and see what we can learn and find!

What is a seashell?

A seashells is the home for the ocean creature that built it. They come in all kind of shapes, colors, sizes and patterns.
They are made with calcium carbonate which makes up the hard protective shell. It protects the ocean creature that lives inside the shell.

Many times the color of the shell is determined by what the creature eats. That is why shells come in all different colors.
Many people enjoy finding seashells that wash up on the beach to collect.

People that collect shells are called a seashell collector and people who enjoy the study of shells are called a conchologist.

Who lives in a seashell?

Mollusks are a group of animals that live in the shells they create. The shell is the home of the live animal. It's pretty amazing. The bigger they grow the bigger the shell grows.

Mollusks use their shells as their house to protect them from danger and prey. When an animal dies they leave behind their beautiful shell that often wash up on the beach for you to find.

Empty shells also provide homes for stowaways like hermit crabs who can't make their own shell to live in.

There are 3 common types of Mollusks groups.

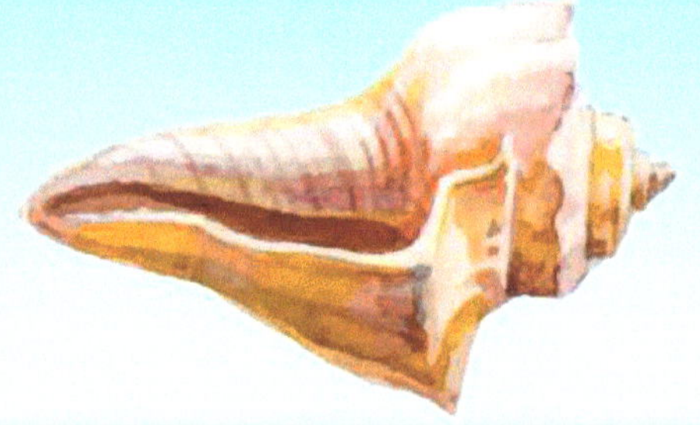

Gastropods are mollusks that live in a single shell such as sea snails like a conch. They use their muscular body to move. Some can even live in freshwater!

Bivalves are mollusks that live in 2 shells that are hinged together like a clam and mussels. They bury at the bottom of ocean floors or lakes.

Cephalopods are mollusks that have a set of arms or tentacles like a squid, octopus or nautilus.

Let's begin our beach shelling adventure from A to Z!

A

Alphabet cone

is for an alphabet cone like me! Alphabet cones are venomous gastropods and have cone shaped shells with brown markings. They have poisonous glands that can actually sting humans. If you find one on the beach, make sure it's empty before you pick it up.

Fun fact: They get their name because the markings can look like letters of the alphabet and even numbers.

Location: These can be commonly found along the gulf coast of Florida.

B

Blue Mussels

The blue mussel is a bivalve that is a filter feeder, which means they filter the ocean water that helps keep the ocean clean. Their shells are a rounded triangle with 2 sides and a hinge that opens and closes. They live in beds that contain lots of mussels that grow close together.

Fun fact: They are abundant and are harvested as a food source for many people around the world.

Location: They can be found all along the North American Coast and all over the world.

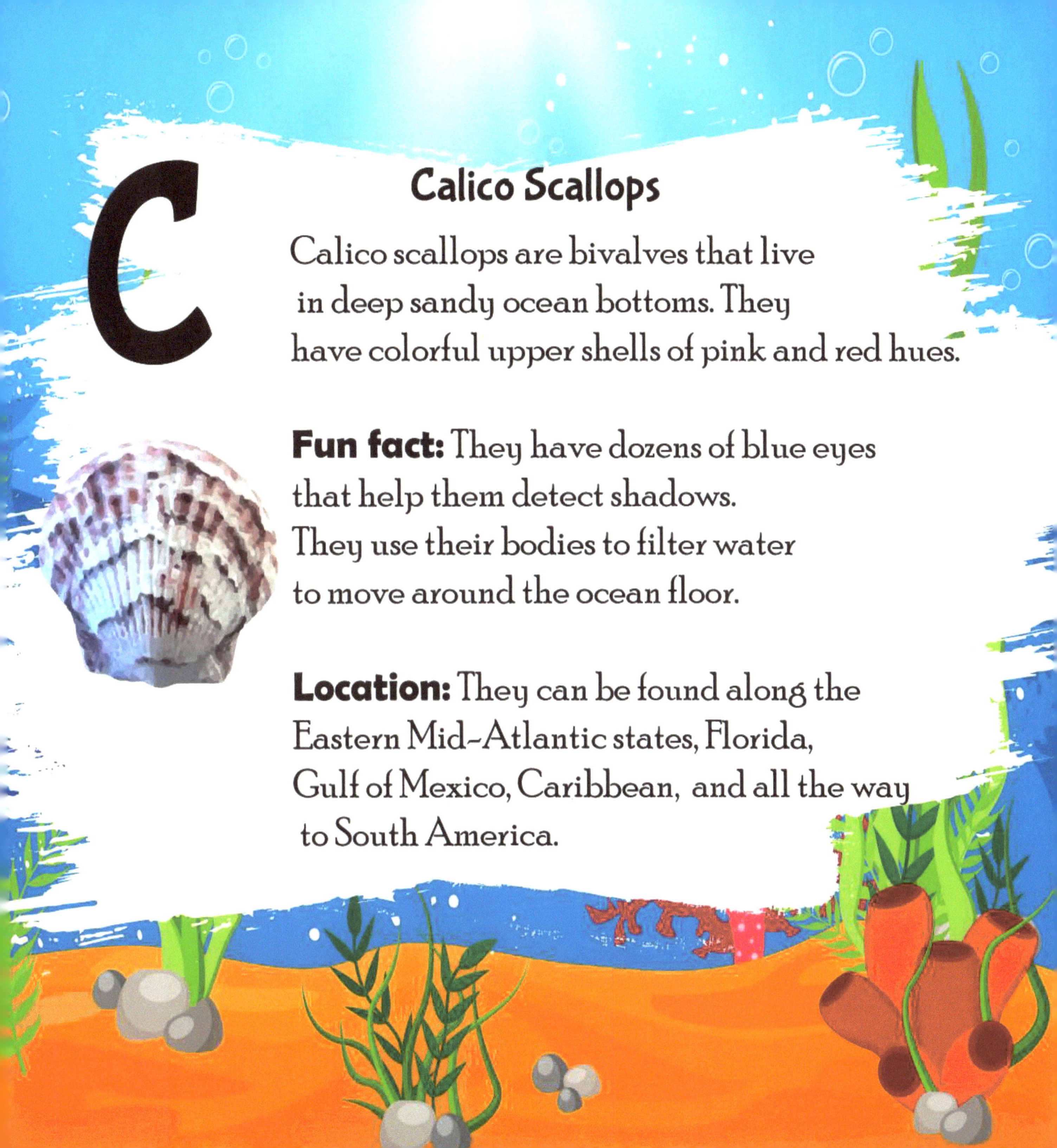

C

Calico Scallops

Calico scallops are bivalves that live in deep sandy ocean bottoms. They have colorful upper shells of pink and red hues.

Fun fact: They have dozens of blue eyes that help them detect shadows. They use their bodies to filter water to move around the ocean floor.

Location: They can be found along the Eastern Mid-Atlantic states, Florida, Gulf of Mexico, Caribbean, and all the way to South America.

Dosinia

Dosinia is a type of saltwater clam.
There are several types of dosinia
clams such as the disk dosinia
and the elegant dosinia.

Fun fact: Fossils of dosinia shells can be
found all over the world and have
been around for over 99 million years.

Location: They live in the sandy bottom
of the ocean. Although they are
found in many places around the world,
they are commonly found in the
Gulf of Mexico and wash ashore south
west Florida.

Egg Casings

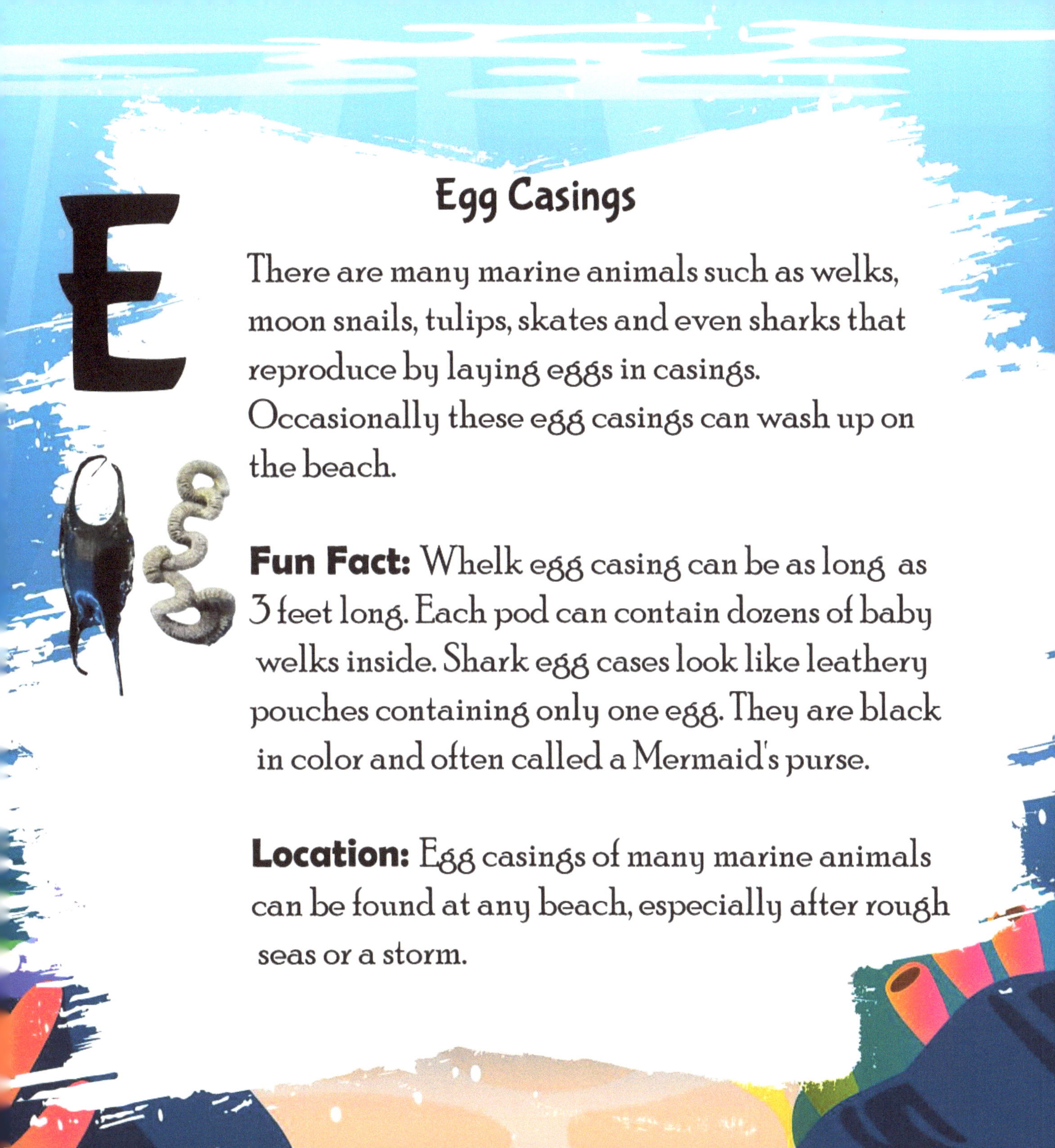

There are many marine animals such as welks, moon snails, tulips, skates and even sharks that reproduce by laying eggs in casings. Occasionally these egg casings can wash up on the beach.

Fun Fact: Whelk egg casing can be as long as 3 feet long. Each pod can contain dozens of baby welks inside. Shark egg cases look like leathery pouches containing only one egg. They are black in color and often called a Mermaid's purse.

Location: Egg casings of many marine animals can be found at any beach, especially after rough seas or a storm.

Florida Horse Conch

Wow, that is big! The Florida horse conch is the biggest saltwater snail in North America and the second biggest in the world next to the Australian trumpet shell. It can get to be about two feet in length. They eat other mollusks such as welks and tulip snails and have an orange and red body.

Fun Fact: The Florida Horse Conch is the state shell of Florida. The shells were used to make tools by Native Americans.

Location: They live in shallow waters from Florida to Mexico.

G

Giant Heart Cockle

These Atlantic giant cockles are one of the largest bivalves that live in shallow water. They can reach up to 6 inches in length and can leap by using their foot to get away from predators.

Fun fact: They get their common name from the appearance when the top and bottom shells are put together. Their shells are symmetrical and appear as a heart when looking at it from it's side.

Location: They live on sandy bottoms from Virginia to Texas. Many other types of cockles can be found around the world.

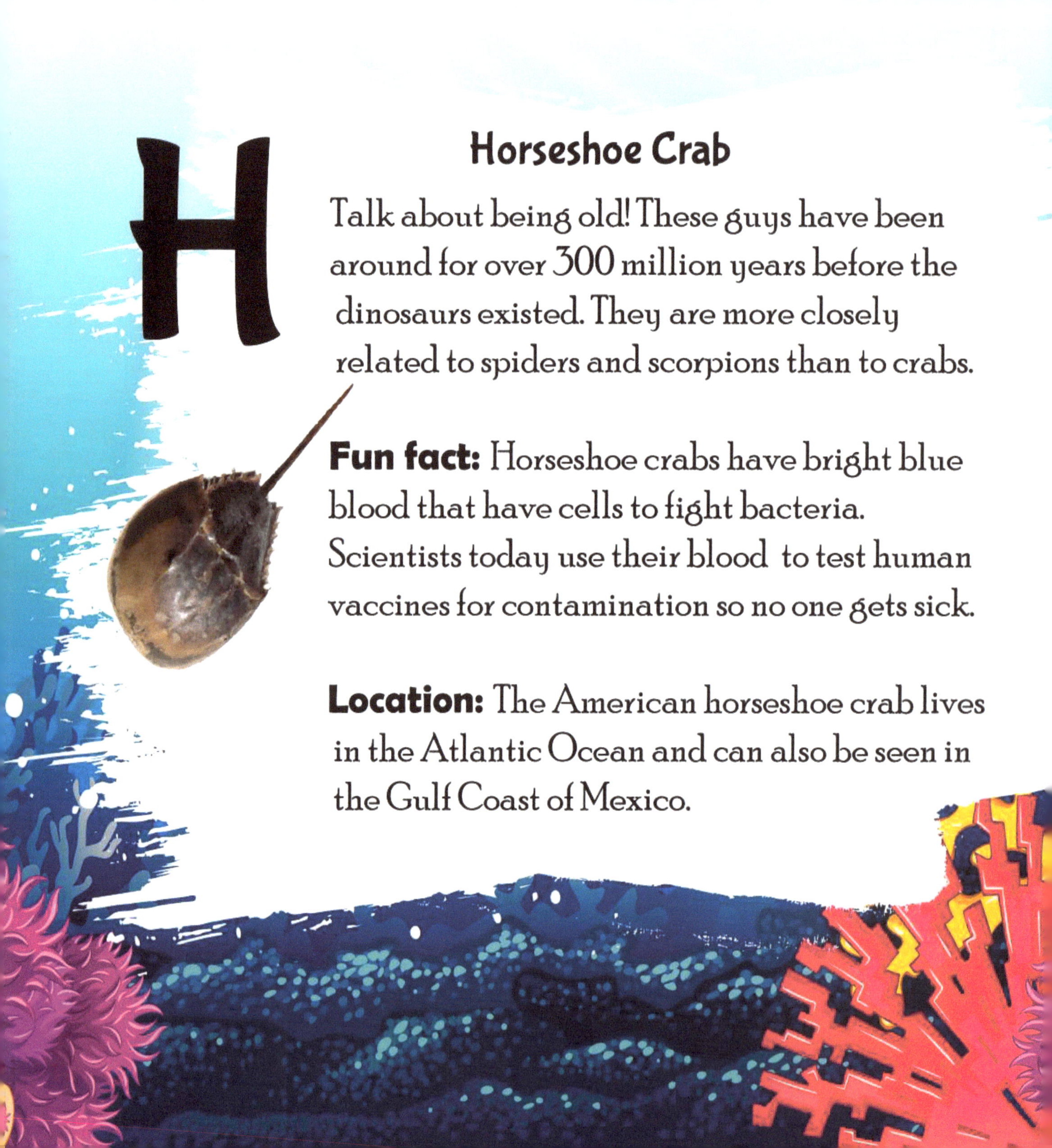

Horseshoe Crab

Talk about being old! These guys have been around for over 300 million years before the dinosaurs existed. They are more closely related to spiders and scorpions than to crabs.

Fun fact: Horseshoe crabs have bright blue blood that have cells to fight bacteria. Scientists today use their blood to test human vaccines for contamination so no one gets sick.

Location: The American horseshoe crab lives in the Atlantic Ocean and can also be seen in the Gulf Coast of Mexico.

Imperial Venus

Imperial Venus clams are bivalves that can get to be about 1½" in size.
They have thick shells with chunky ribs on the shell.

Location: They live in deep water off the shores of Eastern and South America. They can be found from North Carolina to Brazil. You can often find these shells on beaches that have been replenished.

Junonia

Junonia snails live in the deep depths of the ocean. Although they are common, they rarely wash ashore which makes them a rare prized shell find. Their shells typically are cream colored with brown spots. The snail inside the shell moves around by using their foot.

Fun Fact: If you are lucky enough to find an Junonia shell or even a piece of shell you are in the club. This is known to shellers as the "J" Club.

Location: They live in deep waters and are commonly found in the Gulf of Mexico and southwest Florida.

K

Knobbed Whelk

The knobbed whelk is the state shell of New Jersey. They have a beautiful pear shaped spiral shell with knobs. They are a type of sea snail called gastropods.
They can live up to 40 years old.

Fun Fact: They have poor eyesight so they use their smell to locate prey for their next meal.

Location: They are commonly found on the Atlantic coast of the United States.

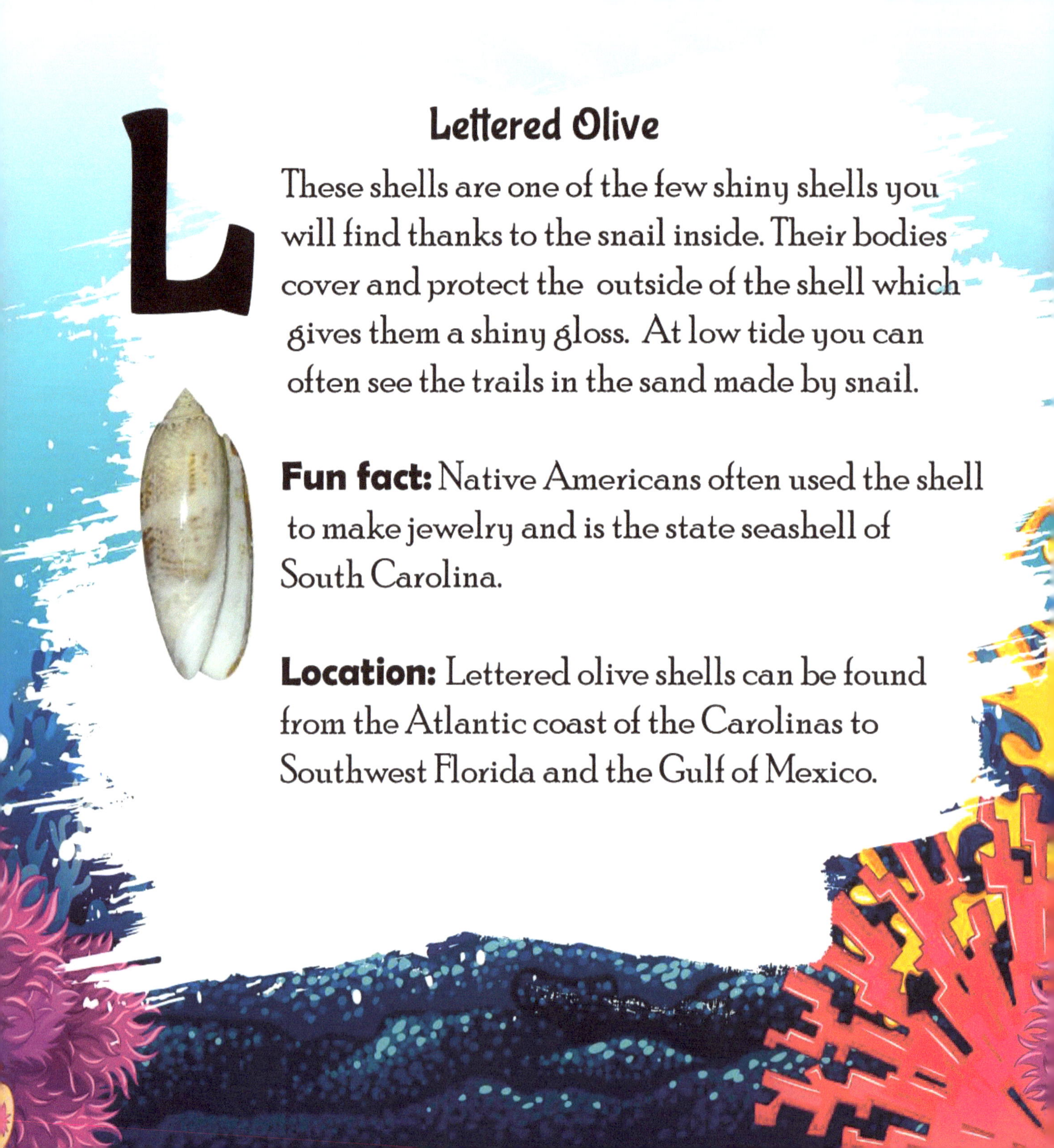

Lettered Olive

These shells are one of the few shiny shells you will find thanks to the snail inside. Their bodies cover and protect the outside of the shell which gives them a shiny gloss. At low tide you can often see the trails in the sand made by snail.

Fun fact: Native Americans often used the shell to make jewelry and is the state seashell of South Carolina.

Location: Lettered olive shells can be found from the Atlantic coast of the Carolinas to Southwest Florida and the Gulf of Mexico.

M

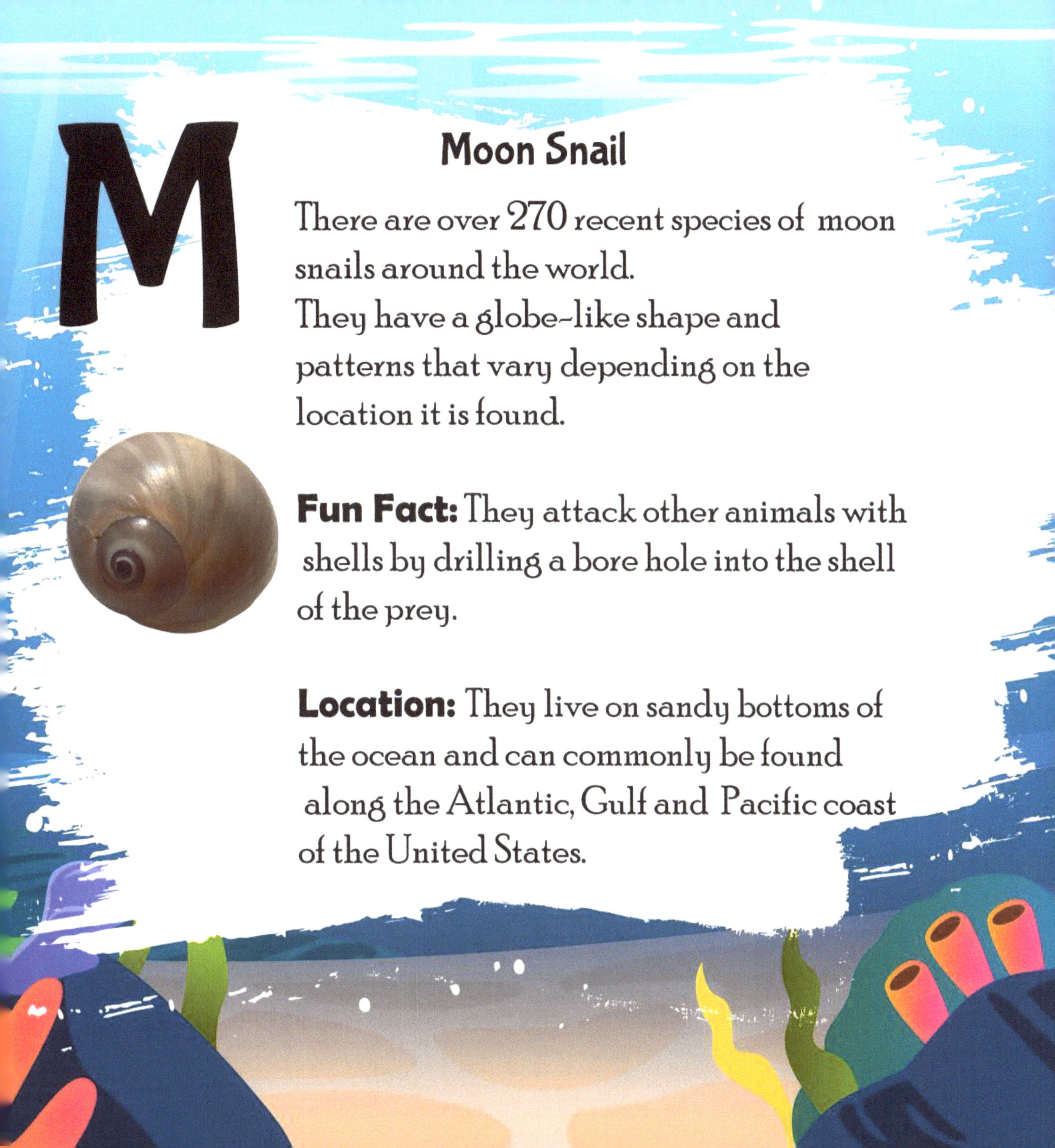

Moon Snail

There are over 270 recent species of moon snails around the world.
They have a globe-like shape and patterns that vary depending on the location it is found.

Fun Fact: They attack other animals with shells by drilling a bore hole into the shell of the prey.

Location: They live on sandy bottoms of the ocean and can commonly be found along the Atlantic, Gulf and Pacific coast of the United States.

Nautilus

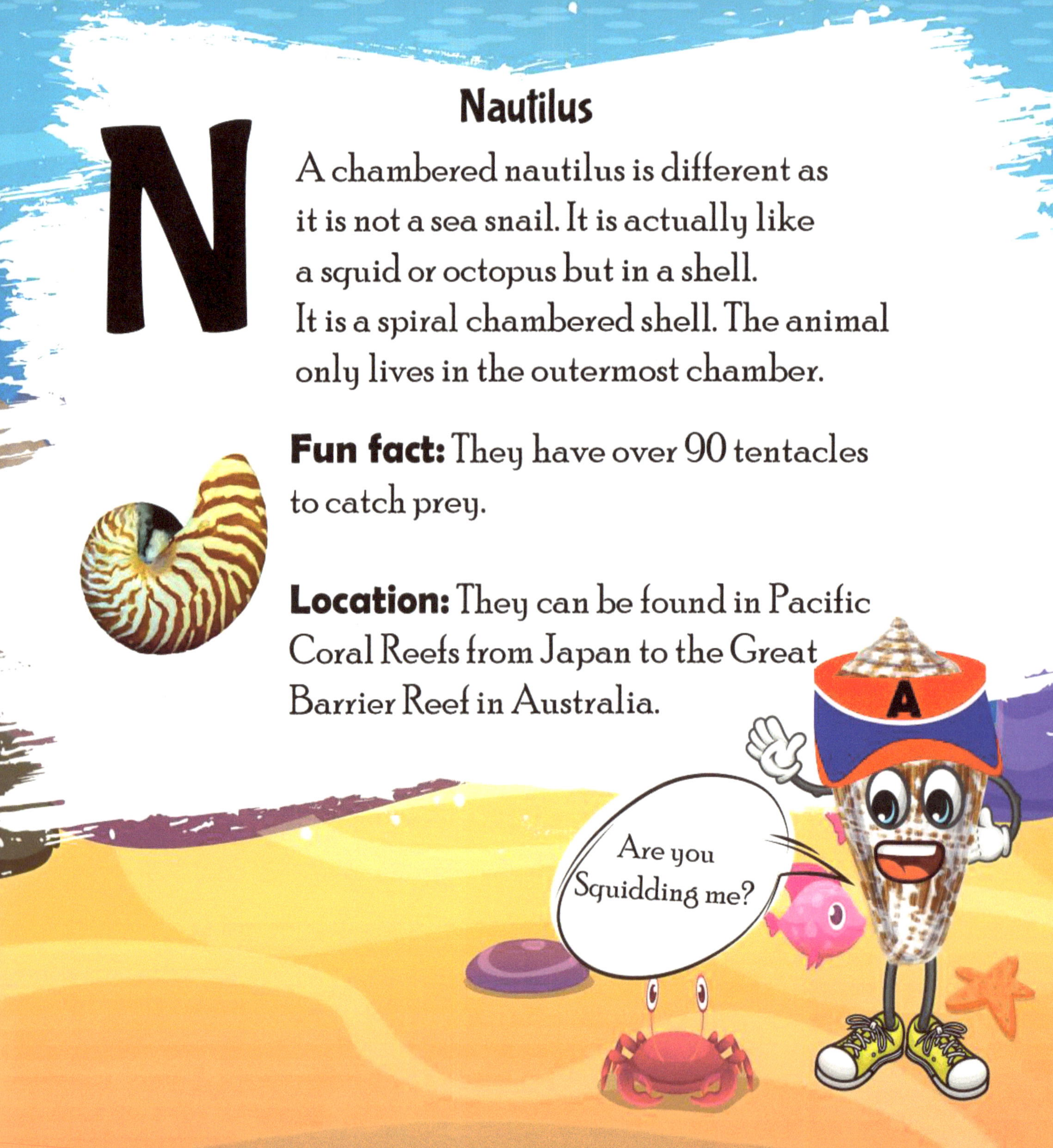

A chambered nautilus is different as it is not a sea snail. It is actually like a squid or octopus but in a shell. It is a spiral chambered shell. The animal only lives in the outermost chamber.

Fun fact: They have over 90 tentacles to catch prey.

Location: They can be found in Pacific Coral Reefs from Japan to the Great Barrier Reef in Australia.

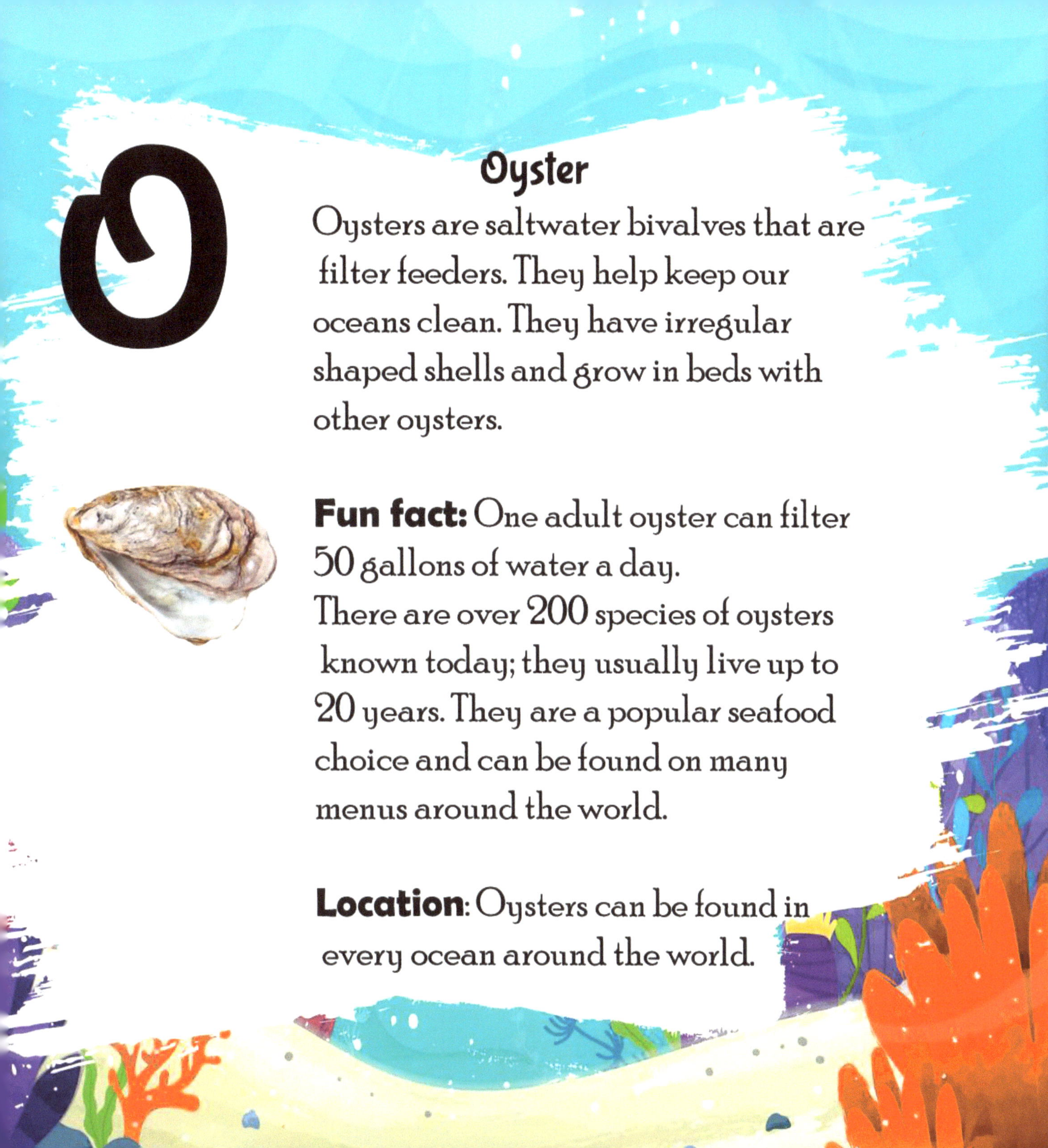

Oyster

Oysters are saltwater bivalves that are filter feeders. They help keep our oceans clean. They have irregular shaped shells and grow in beds with other oysters.

Fun fact: One adult oyster can filter 50 gallons of water a day.
There are over 200 species of oysters known today; they usually live up to 20 years. They are a popular seafood choice and can be found on many menus around the world.

Location: Oysters can be found in every ocean around the world.

Pollution

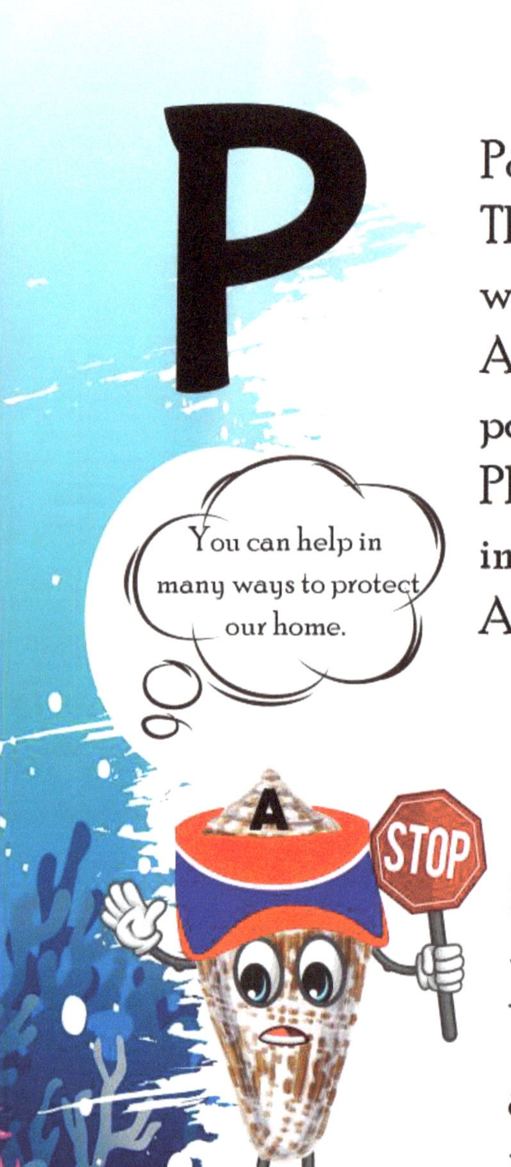

Pollution is the number one killer of our oceans. There are several types of pollutants that enter our waters like chemicals, plastics, and garbage. All pollution comes from the land. Fertilizers and pesticides runoff into the ocean and kill marine life. Plastics are mistaken for food and are mistakenly ingested by sea turtles and other marine life. All sorts of garbage is dumped into the seas.

Not so fun fact: Every minute about 2 garbage trucks of waste are dumped into our oceans. You can help save my friends by reducing your garbage, reuse what we have and recycle to make new items.

Location: Sadly pollution is everywhere! Make a difference and do your part to help our ocean and planet.

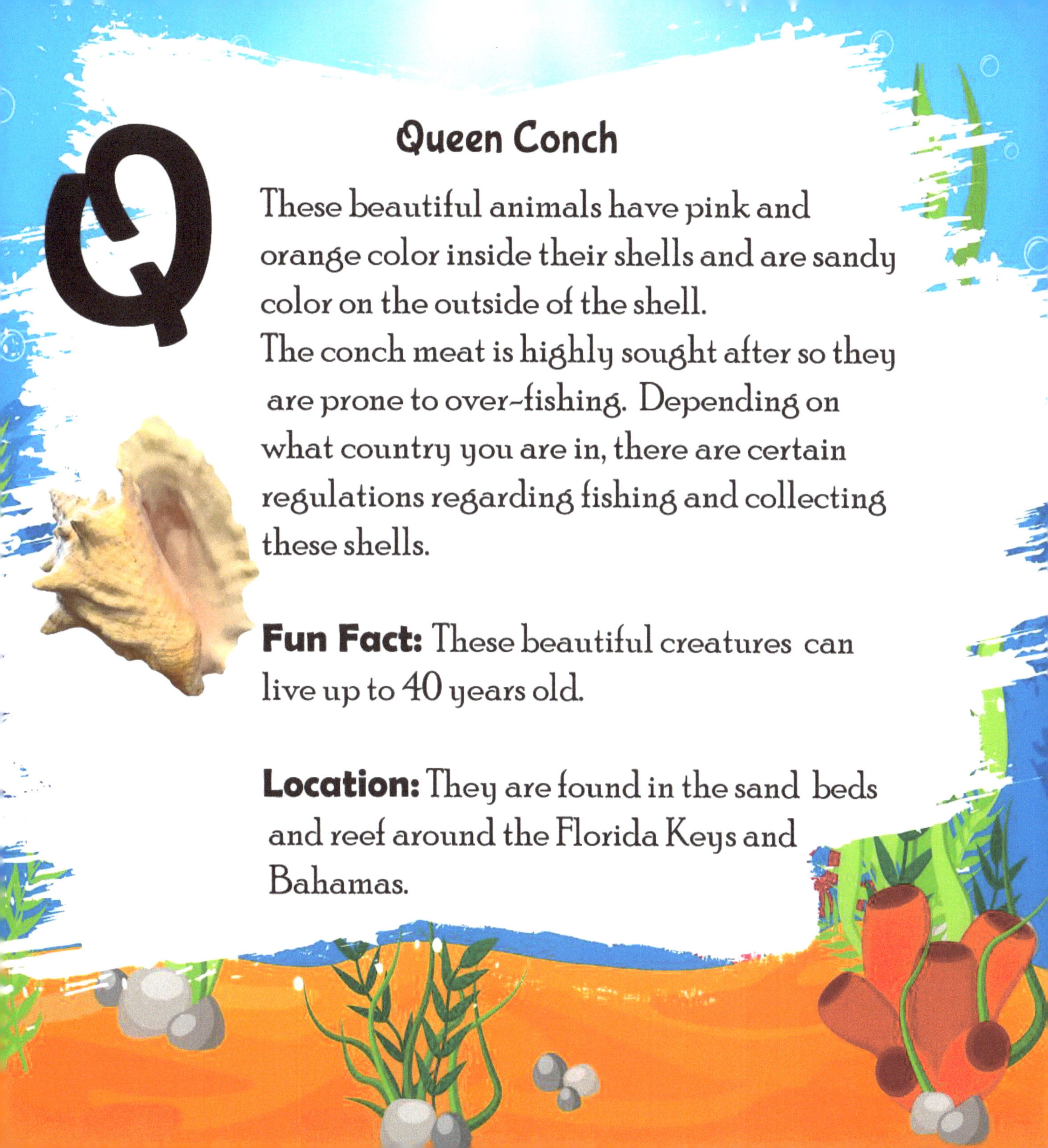

Queen Conch

These beautiful animals have pink and orange color inside their shells and are sandy color on the outside of the shell.
The conch meat is highly sought after so they are prone to over-fishing. Depending on what country you are in, there are certain regulations regarding fishing and collecting these shells.

Fun Fact: These beautiful creatures can live up to 40 years old.

Location: They are found in the sand beds and reef around the Florida Keys and Bahamas.

R

Rock Snails

These are saltwater snails that are part of the Murex family. They feed on oysters and mussels. They need rocks to thrive.
They are not commonly found on beaches that do not have rock pilings.

.

Fun Fact: They attack prey in groups and have teeth.

Location: They can be found in oceans around the world.

Sand Dollar

There are many varieties of sand dollars. They are flat sea urchins that live on the seabed. They are covered in tiny hairs that help them move across the ocean floor.

Fun Fact: If you break open a dried up sand dollar, you can see what looks like tiny doves which are actually their teeth.

Location: Sand dollars can be found around the world. They can often be found in Florida as well as along the coastlines of North America.

T

Tulip Shell

There are several different species of tulip snails. They are large predatory snails that can grow to between 2 to 9 inches.

Fun Fact: The shape of their shell look like an closed tulip.

Location: These attractive shells can be found in Florida along the Gulf Coast of Mexico and the Northern Caribbean Sea.

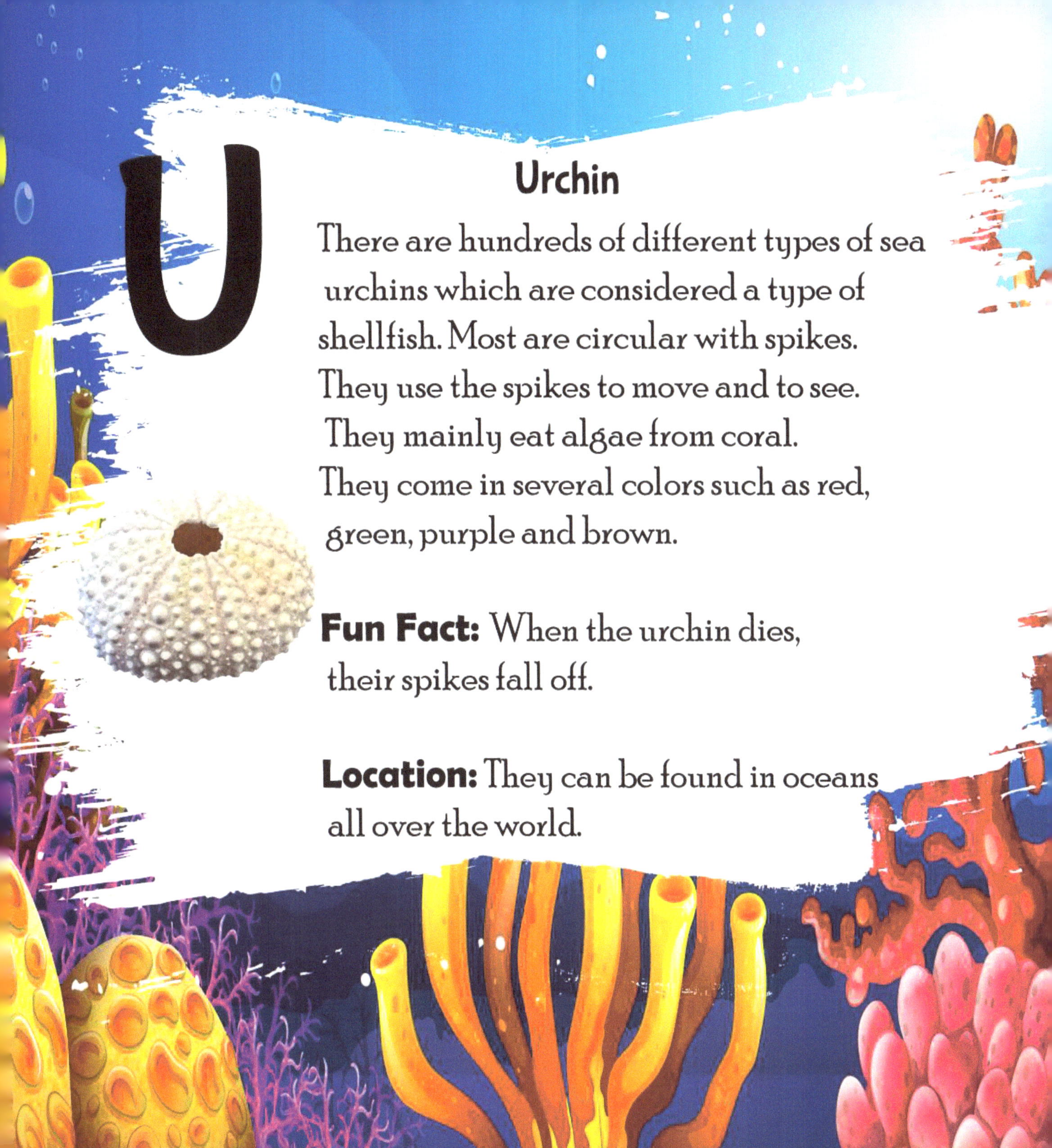

Urchin

There are hundreds of different types of sea urchins which are considered a type of shellfish. Most are circular with spikes. They use the spikes to move and to see. They mainly eat algae from coral. They come in several colors such as red, green, purple and brown.

Fun Fact: When the urchin dies, their spikes fall off.

Location: They can be found in oceans all over the world.

Violet Snail

Another name for the violet snail is the janthina. These snails actually float on the surface of the ocean in large groups. Their pretty purple shells are one of the most delicate.

Fun fact: They make air bubbles so they can drift on the ocean surface.

Location: They live in warm tropical waters like the Atlantic, Caribbean, Pacific and Indian oceans. During high winds you can often find them washed ashore.

W

Wentletrap

These small off white shells are sometimes called ladder or staircase shells. Some are super tiny and others can be a few inches in size depending on the species.

Fun Fact: In Dutch, the name wentletrap means spiral staircase.

Location: They are found all over the world in every ocean.

X

X Marks The Spot

Arrgh, Treasure! The X mark found on beaches or on a map could indicate where genuine Spanish and pirate treasures can be found. It can be tricky to spot but a metal detector can be helpful, especially after a storm.

Fun Fact: On the Gold Coast of Florida, 112 ships of the Spanish Fleet of 1715 sunk in a storm. Most of the treasure is still undiscovered. Artifacts still wash up today on the beaches.

Location: Sunken ships all over the world.

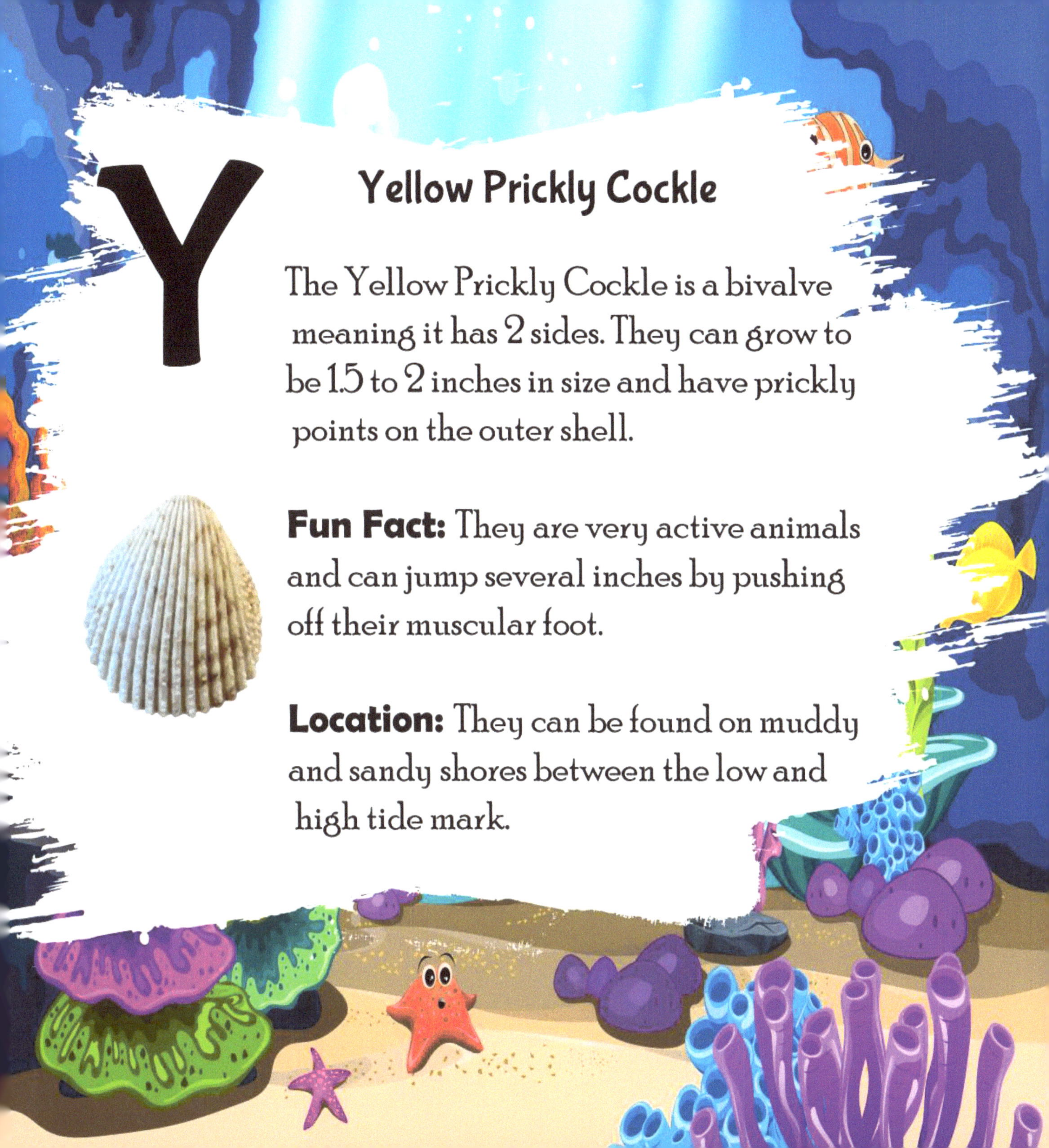

Y

Yellow Prickly Cockle

The Yellow Prickly Cockle is a bivalve meaning it has 2 sides. They can grow to be 1.5 to 2 inches in size and have prickly points on the outer shell.

Fun Fact: They are very active animals and can jump several inches by pushing off their muscular foot.

Location: They can be found on muddy and sandy shores between the low and high tide mark.

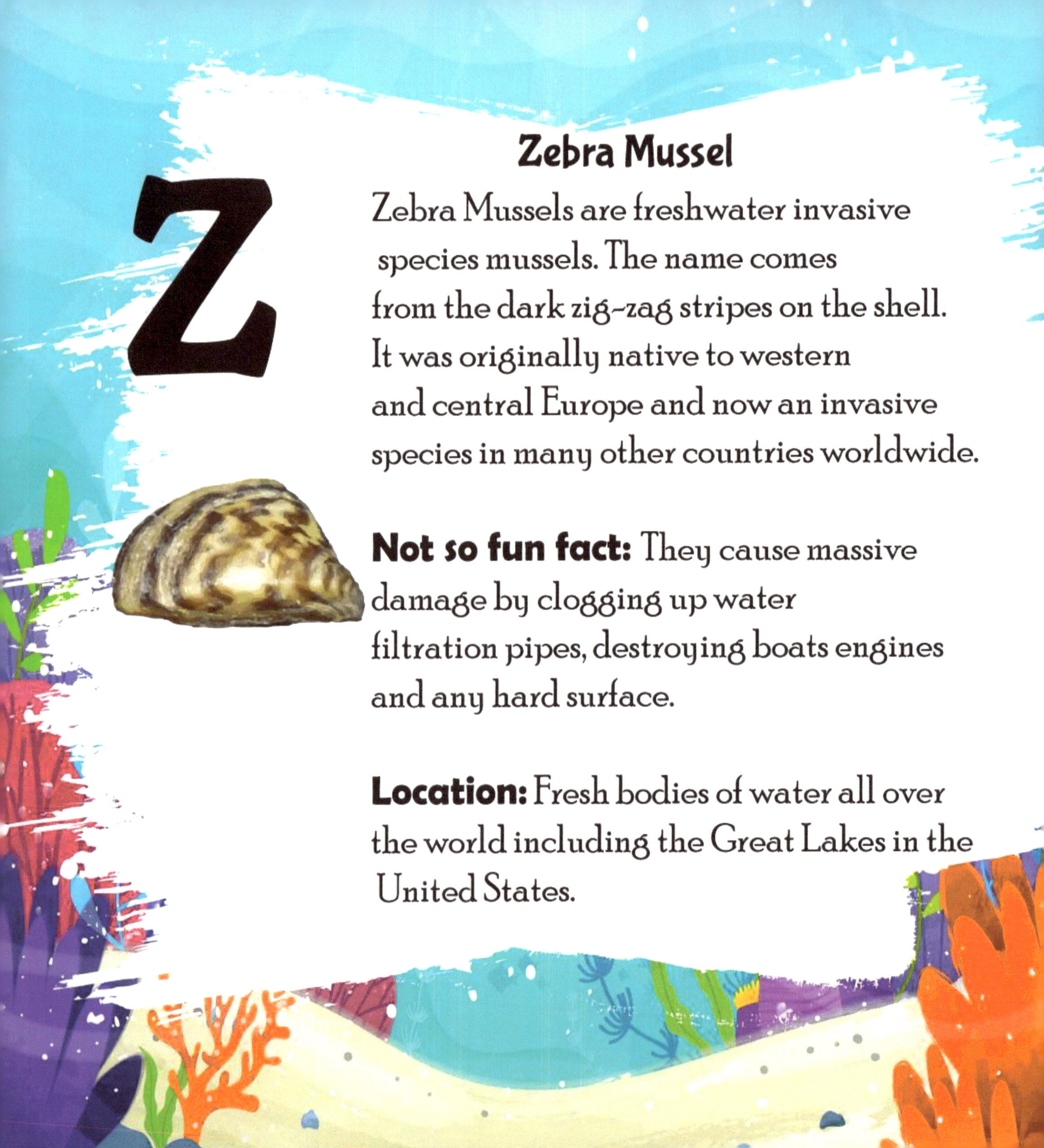

Zebra Mussel

Zebra Mussels are freshwater invasive species mussels. The name comes from the dark zig-zag stripes on the shell. It was originally native to western and central Europe and now an invasive species in many other countries worldwide.

Not so fun fact: They cause massive damage by clogging up water filtration pipes, destroying boats engines and any hard surface.

Location: Fresh bodies of water all over the world including the Great Lakes in the United States.

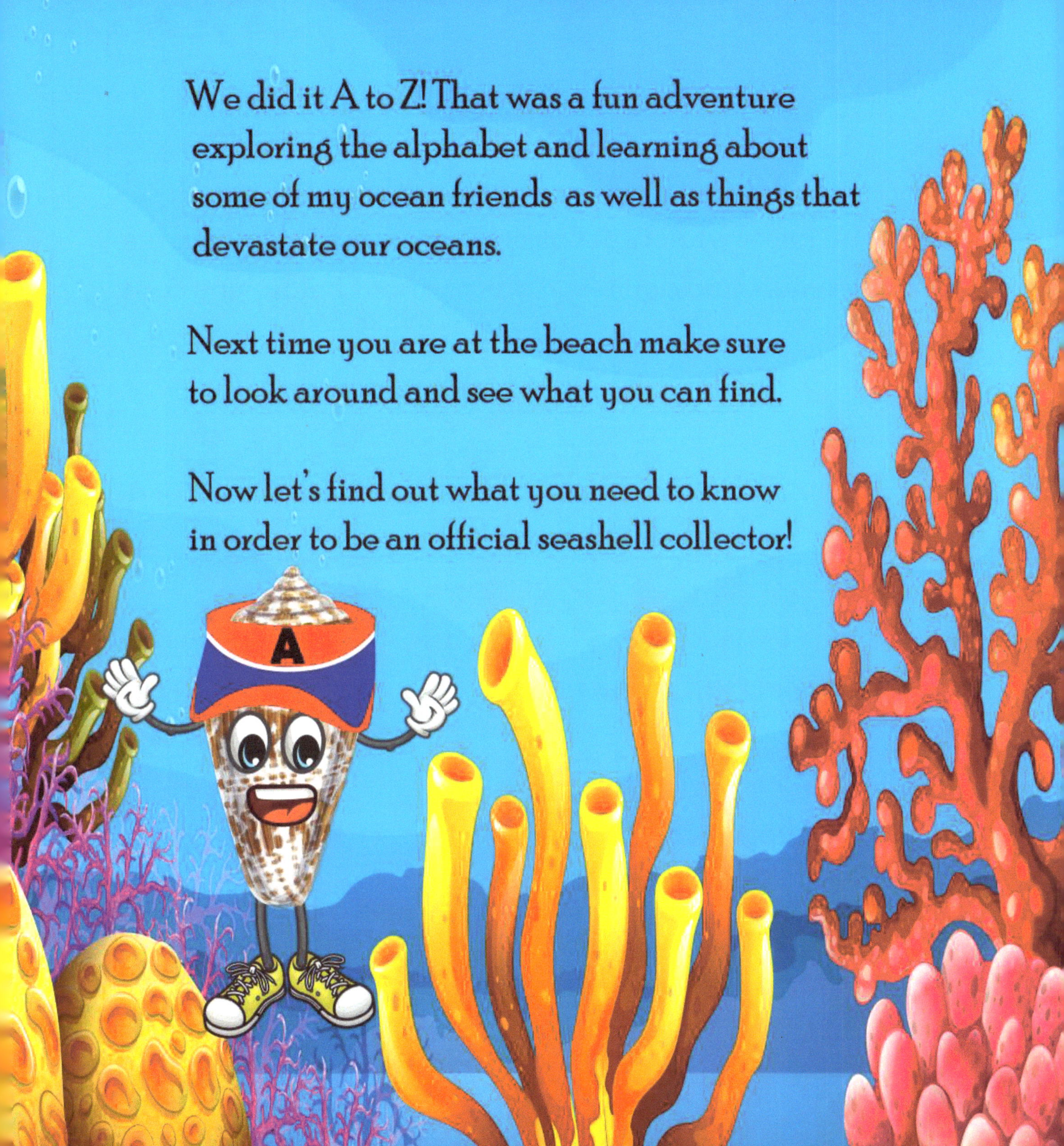

We did it A to Z! That was a fun adventure exploring the alphabet and learning about some of my ocean friends as well as things that devastate our oceans.

Next time you are at the beach make sure to look around and see what you can find.

Now let's find out what you need to know in order to be an official seashell collector!

How to become an Official Seashell Collector!

You are on your way to becoming an official Seashell Collector! Now you know what types of shells to look for, here are a few supplies, rules, and dangers to know about before you start.

What to Pack

- Shelling bag to put your treasures in and containers for delicate seashells.

- Extra bag to pick up any beach trash others left behind. My ocean friends will thank you!

- Shovel or sand sifter to help pick up shells on the water's edge.

- Bottle of water because it can get really hot.

- Sunscreen and hat to protect you from the sun.

Shelling Rules

There are a few rules my friends would like you to follow to protect our homes and environment.

• Never take home shells with live animals inside. Although most shells wash ashore empty, sometimes they wash up alive depending on the tides. If they are alive it should be returned back to the ocean.

• Always fill in the holes you dig on the beach so no one gets hurt.

• Don't leave behind trash. Trash is our enemy and ends up in our oceans.

• Make sure there are no shelling restrictions in the area you are shelling.

• Don't take all the shells, leave some behind for other shellers or sea creatures looking for a new home.

• Most Importantly- HAVE FUN!

Dangers

The beach is full of so much fun sometimes we forget it's not always safe. It's important to be aware of a few things so you don't get hurt.

Tides

Be aware of your surroundings and the tides. Is it low or high tide? Check the tides before you go on long walks. Sometimes you can access areas at low tide that you can not walk when it's high tide. If you get stuck with the high tide you may not be able to get back to your starting point.

Rip tides

These are dangerous tides that can pull someone out to sea. If the waves don't look normal to you or the lifeguards have rip tide flags up, don't go in the water even knee deep.

Weather

Always check the weather and ocean conditions. Never go out to the beach in a lightning and thunderstorm. If a storm is approaching it's best to leave.

Animals

There are many live animals that can bite or sting such as jellyfish, crabs and sharks. Some dangerous mollusks also live in shells, so be sure to check the shells before picking them up. Although the beach is very pretty, it has some dangers so beware of these to stay safe.

Congratulations! You are now an official Seashell Collector! That's Sheller-rific! Read the below pledge with me.

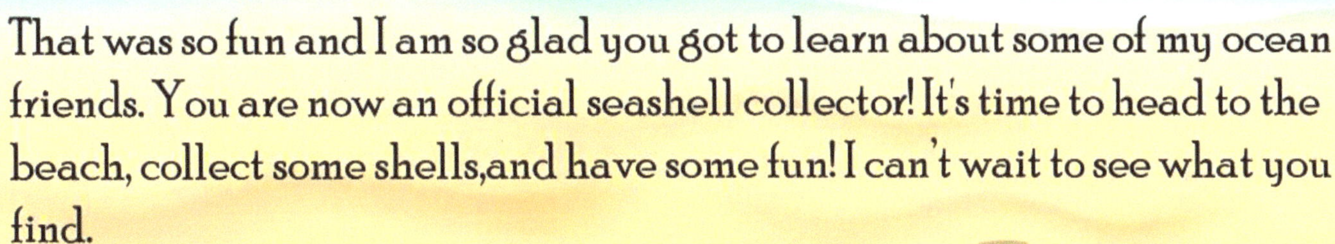

Artie's Official Seashell Collector Pledge

I promise to collect shells that are empty
Only observe live animals
Keep my ocean friends safe
Be aware of danger
And have fun.

That was so fun and I am so glad you got to learn about some of my ocean friends. You are now an official seashell collector! It's time to head to the beach, collect some shells, and have some fun! I can't wait to see what you find.

I will see you again next time as I go on more adventures, meeting new friends as I find my way home to Cone City. Have a Shell-Tastic day shelling!

Shell Guide A to Z

Alphabet cone

Blue Mussels

Calico Scallops

Dosinia

Egg Casings

Florida Horse Conch

Giant Heart Cockle

Horseshoe Crab

Imperial Venus

Junonia

Knobbed Whelk

Lettered Olive

Moon Snail

Nautilus

Oyster

Pollution

Queen Conch

Rock Snails

Sand Dollar

Tulip Shell

Urchin

Violet Snail

Wenteltrap

X marks the spot- Treasure

Yellow Prickly Cockle

Zebra Mussel

Shelling Log

Date____________

Shell Name: ____________________________________
Location: ______________________________________
Weather: ______________________________________
Found by: ______________________________________

Date____________

Shell Name: ____________________________________
Location: ______________________________________
Weather: ______________________________________
Found by: ______________________________________

Date____________

Shell Name: ____________________________________
Location: ______________________________________
Weather: ______________________________________
Found by: ______________________________________

Date____________

Shell Name: ____________________________________
Location: ______________________________________
Weather: ______________________________________
Found by: ______________________________________

www.ingramcontent.com/pod-product-compliance
Lightning Source LLC
Chambersburg PA
CBHW040147240726
48664CB00002B/626